The
Awakened Soul

ISBN: 1 86476 081 8

AXIOM
AUSTRALIA

Printed in Malaysia

The image used on pages 5 - 128 was obtained from IMSI's Masterclips Collection, 75 Rowland Way, Novato, CA 94945, USA

The Awakened Soul

Selections from
Kahlil Gibran

A child in the womb, no sooner born than returned to the earth – such is the fate of man, the fate of nations and of the sun, the moon, and the stars.

Are you a soldier compelled by the harsh law of man to forsake wife and children, and go forth into the field of battle for the sake of Greed, which your leaders mis-call Duty?

Braving obstacles and hardships is nobler than retreat to tranquillity. The butterfly that hovers around the lamp until it dies is more admirable than the mole that lives in a dark tunnel.

Every young man remembers his first love and tries to recapture that strange hour, the memory of which changes his deepest feeling and makes him so happy in spite of all the bitterness of its mystery.

Humans are divided into different clans and tribes, and belong to countries and towns. But I find myself a stranger to all communities and belong to no settlement. The universe is my country and the human family is my tribe.

Men are weak, and it is sad that they divide among themselves. The world is narrow and it is unwise to cleave it into kingdoms, empires, and provinces.

I would be the least among men with dreams and the desire to fulfil them, rather than the greatest with no dreams and no desires.

If you sing beauty, though alone in the heart of the desert, you will have an audience.

It is indeed misery if I stretch an empty hand to men and receive nothing; but it is hopelessness if I stretch a full hand and find none to receive.

Limited love asks for possession of the beloved, but the unlimited asks only for itself.

My soul preached to me and said, "Do not be delighted because of praise, and do not be distressed because of blame."

Ere my soul counselled me, I doubted the worth of my work.

Now I realise that the trees blossom in Spring and bear fruit in Summers without seeking praise; and they drop their leaves in Autumn and become naked in Winter without fearing blame.

Paradise is there, behind that door, in the next room;
but I have lost the key.
Perhaps I have only mislaid it.

Sadness is but a wall between two gardens.

Strange, the desire for certain pleasures is a part of my pain.

He who has not looked on Sorrow will never see Joy.

The obvious is that which is never seen until someone expresses it simply.

There is a desire deep within the soul which drives man from the seen to the unseen, to philosophy and to the divine.

Those who give you a serpent when you ask for a fish may have nothing but serpents to give. It is then generosity on their part.

What man is capable of leaving an edifice on whose construction he has spent all his life, even though that edifice is his own prison? It is difficult to get rid of it in one day.

Whoever would be a teacher of men let him begin by teaching himself before teaching others; and let him teach by example before teaching by word. For he who teaches himself and rectifies his own ways is more deserving of respect and reverence than he who would teach others and rectify their ways.

You may deprive me of my possessions; you may shed my blood and burn my body, but you cannot hurt my spirit or touch my truth.

A disagreement may be the shortest cut between two minds.

Art is one step from the visibly known toward the unknown.

Crime is either another name of need or an aspect of a disease.

Faith is an oasis in the heart which will never be reached by the caravan of thinking.

He who repeats what he does not understand is no better that an ass that is loaded with books.

The truly just is he who feels half guilty of your misdeeds.

Old age is the snow of the earth; it must, through light and truth, give warmth to the seeds of youth below, protecting them and fulfilling their purpose.

When you tell your trouble to your neighbour you present him with a part of your heart. If he possesses a great soul, he thanks you; if he possesses a small one, he belittles you.

Keep me away from the wisdom which does not cry, the philosophy which does not laugh and the greatness which does not bow before children.

In the house of Ignorance there is no mirror in which to view your soul.

Love that does not renew itself every day becomes a habit and in turn a slavery.

If there is such a thing as sin, some of us commit it backward following our forefathers' footsteps;
And some of us commit it forward by overruling our children.

I have learned silence from the talkative, toleration from the intolerant, and kindness from the unkind; yet, strange, I am ungrateful to those teachers.

How can I lose faith in the justice of life, when the dreams of those who sleep upon feathers are not more beautiful than the dreams of those who sleep upon the earth?

God has given you a spirit with wings on which to soar into the spacious firmament of Love and Freedom. Is it not pitiful then that you cut your wings with your own hands and suffer your soul to crawl like an insect upon the earth?

Do not be merciful, but be just, for mercy is bestowed upon the guilty criminal, while justice is all that an innocent man requires.

Beauty is that harmony between joy and sorrow which begins in our holy of holies and ends beyond the scope of our imagination.

A pearl is a temple built by pain around a grain of sand.

What longing built our bodies and around what grains?

Wit is often a mask. If you could tear it you would find either a genius irritated or cleverness juggling.

You see but your shadow when you turn your back to the sun.

When I stood a clear mirror before you, you gazed into me and saw your image.

Then you said, "I love you." But in truth you loved yourself in me.

Trees are poems that the earth writes upon the sky. We fell them down and turn them into paper that we may record our emptiness.

They say to me, "You must needs choose between the pleasures of this world and the peace of the next world." And I say to them, "I have chosen both the delights of this world and the peace of the next. For I know in my heart that the Supreme Poet wrote but one poem, and it scans perfectly, and it also rhymes perfectly."

There is no struggle of soul and body save in the minds of those whose souls are asleep and whose bodies are out of tune.

The silence of the envious is too noisy.

The fool sees naught but folly; and the madman only madness. Yesterday I asked a foolish man to count the fools among us. He laughed and said, "This is too hard a thing to do, and it will take too long. Were it not better to count only the wise?"

Should we all confess our sins to one another we would laugh at one another for our lack of originality.

Persecution cannot harm him who stands by Truth. Did not Socrates fall proudly a victim in body? Was not Paul stoned for the sake of the Truth? It is our inner self that hurts us when we disobey and kills us when we betray.

Oftentimes I have hated in self-defence; but if I were stronger I would not have used such a weapon.

Love is the only freedom in the world because it so elevates the spirit that the laws of humanity and the phenomena of nature do not alter its course.

Strange that you should pity the slow-footed and not the slow-minded,
And the blind-eyed rather than the blind-hearted.

It was but yesterday I thought myself a fragment quivering without rhythm in the sphere of life. Now I know that I am the sphere, and all life in rhythmic fragments moves within me.

In battling evil, excess is good; for he who is moderate in announcing the truth is presenting half-truth. He conceals the other half out of fear of the people's wrath.

If some fool tells you the soul perishes like the body and that which dies never returns, tell him the flower perishes but the seed remains and lies before us as the secret of life everlasting.

Hell is not in torture;
Hell is in an empty heart.

I had a second birth when my soul and by body loved
one another and were married.

Generosity is not in giving me that which I need more that you do, but it is in giving me that which you need more than I do.

Despair weakens our sight and closes our ears. We can see nothing but spectres of doom, and can hear only the beating of our agitated hearts.

A madman is not less a musician than you or myself; only the instrument on which he plays is a little out of tune.

Be not satisfied with partial contentment, for he who engulfs the spring of life with one empty jar will depart with two full jars.

You owe more than gold to him who serves you. Give him of your heart or serve him.

When God threw me, a pebble, into this wondrous lake I disturbed its surface with countless circles. But when I reached the depths I became very still.

To be modest in speaking truth is hypocrisy.

Wisdom is not in words;
Wisdom is meaning within words.

The significance of man is not in what he attains, but rather in what he longs to attain.

There is neither religion nor science beyond beauty.

The reality of the other person is not in what he reveals to you, but in what he cannot reveal to you.

Therefore, if you would understand him, listen not to what he says but rather to what he does not say.

Seven times have I despised my soul:

The first time when I saw her being meek that she might attain height.

The second time when I saw her limping before the crippled.

The third time when she was given to choose between the hard and the easy, and she chose the easy.

The fourth time when she committed a wrong, and comforted herself that others also commit wrong.

The fifth time when she forbore for weakness, and attributed her patience to strength.

The sixth time when she despised the ugliness of a face, and knew not that it was one of her own masks.

And the seventh time when she sang a song of praise, and deemed it a virtue.

Perplexity is the beginning of knowledge.

The bitterest thing in our to-day's sorrow is the memory of our yesterday's joy.

Nature reaches out to us with welcoming arms, and bids us enjoy her beauty; but we dread her silence and rush into the crowded cities, there to huddle like sheep fleeing from a ferocious wolf.

It takes two of us to discover truth: one to utter it and one to understand it.

Love and doubt have never been on speaking terms.

If your knowledge teaches you not the value of things, and frees you not from the bondage to matter, you shall never come near the throne of Truth.

If it were not for guests, all houses would be graves.

We often sing lullabies to our children that we ourselves may sleep.

I am ignorant of absolute truth. But I am humble before my ignorance, and therein lies my honour and my reward.

He who understands you is greater kin to you than your own brother. For even your own kindred may neither understand you nor know your true worth.

Desire is half of life; indifference is half of death.

Forgetfulness is a form of freedom.

Be not like him who sits by his fireside and watches the fire go out, then blows vainly upon the dead ashes. Do not give up hope or yield to despair because of that which is past, for to bewail the irretrievable is the worst of human frailties.

A hermit is one who renounces the world of fragments that he may enjoy the world wholly and without interruption.

You may judge others only according to your knowledge of yourself.

Tell me now, who among us is guilty and who is unguilty?

When either your joy or your sorrow becomes great the world becomes small.

Wisdom ceases to be wisdom when it becomes too proud to weep, too grave to laugh, and too self-full to see other than itself.

Thoughts have a higher dwelling place than the visible world, and its skies are not clouded by sensuality. Imagination finds a road to the realm of the gods, and there man can glimpse that which is to be after the soul's liberation from the world of substance.

There is a space between man's imagination and man's attainment that may only be traversed by his longing.

The most talkative is the least intelligent, and there is hardly a difference between an orator and an auctioneer.

Said a philosopher to a street sweeper, "I pity you. Yours is a hard and dirty task."

And the street sweeper said, "Thank you, sir. But tell me, what is your task?"

And the philosopher answered, saying, "I study man's mind, his deeds and his desires."

Then the street sweeper went on with his sweeping and said with a smile, "I pity you too."

Perhaps the sea's definition of a shell is the pearl.
Perhaps time's definition of coal is the diamond.

The appearance of things changes according to the
emotions, and thus we see magic and beauty in them,
while the magic and beauty are really in ourselves.

My soul preached to me and showed me that I am neither more than the pygmy, nor less that the giant. Ere my soul preached to me, I looked upon humanity as two men: one weak, whom I pitied, and the other strong, whom I followed or resisted in defiance.

But now I have learned that I was as both are and made from the same elements. My origin is their origin, my conscience is their conscience, my contention is their contention, and my pilgrimage is their pilgrimage.

If you would rise but a cubit above race and country and self you would indeed become godlike.

Long were you a dream in your mother's sleep, and then she woke to give you birth.

I would not listen to a conqueror preaching to the conquered.

It is the honour of the murdered that he is not the murderer.

I abstain from the people who consider insolence, bravery and tenderness cowardice. And I abstain from those who consider chatter, wisdom and silence ignorance.

The gifted were once proud in serving princes.
Now they claim honour in serving paupers.

The song that lies silent in the heart of a mother sings
upon the lips of her child.

There is something in our life which is nobler and more supreme than fame; and this something is the great deed that invokes fame.

We are all prisoners, but some of us are in cells with windows and some without.

When you have solved all the mysteries of life you long for death, for it is but another mystery of life. Birth and death are the two noblest expressions of bravery.

You may chain my hands and shackle my feet; you may even throw me into a dark prison, but you shall not enslave my thinking because it is free.

Words are timeless. You should utter them or write them with a knowledge of their timelessness.

Your saying to me, "I do not understand you," is praise beyond my worth, and an insult you do not deserve.

A strange form of self-indulgence! There are times when I would be wronged and cheated, that I may laugh at the expense of those who think I do not know I am being wronged and cheated.

Beauty shines brighter in the heart of him who longs for it than in the eyes of him who sees it.

During the ebb, I wrote a line upon the sand,
Committing to it all that is in my soul and mind;
I returned at the tide to read it and to ponder upon it.
I found naught upon the seashore but my ignorance.

Government is an agreement between you and myself. You and myself are often wrong.

In truth you owe naught to any man. You owe all to all men.

How mean am I when life gives me gold and I give you silver, and yet I deem myself generous.

I have never agreed with my other self wholly. The truth of the matter seems to lie between us.

If winter should say. "Spring is in my heart," who would believe winter?

Know your own true worth, and you shall not perish. Reason is your light and your beacon of Truth. Reason is the source of Life.

Man struggles to find life outside himself, unaware that the life he is seeking is within him.

One hour devoted to mourning and lamenting the stolen equality of the weak is nobler than a century filled with greed and usurpation.

Poetry is not an opinion expressed. It is a song that rises from a bleeding wound or a smiling mouth.

Sow a seed and the earth will yield you a flower. Dream your dream to the sky and it will bring you your beloved.

The gifts which derive from justice are greater than those that spring from charity.

The things which the child loves remain in the domain of the heart until old age. The most beautiful thing in life is that our souls remain hovering over the places where we once enjoyed ourselves.

There lies a green field between the scholar and the poet; should the scholar cross it, he becomes a wise man; should the poet cross it, he becomes a prophet.

We choose our joys and our sorrows long before we experience them.

When you long for blessings that you may not name, and when you grieve knowing not the cause, then indeed you are growing with all things that grow, and rising toward your greater self.

You are indeed charitable when you give, and while giving turn your face away so that you may not see the shyness of the receiver.

A traveller am I and a navigator, and every day I discover a new region within my soul.

Believing is a fine thing, but placing those beliefs into execution is a test of strength. Many are those who talk like the roar of the sea, but their lives are shallow and stagnant, like the rotting marshes. Many are those who lift their heads above the mountain tops, but their spirits remain dormant in the obscurity of the caverns.

Each thing that exists remains forever, and the very existence of existence is proof of its eternity. But without that realisation, which is the knowledge of perfect being, man would never know whether there was existence or non-existence. If eternal existence is altered, then it must become more beautiful; and if it disappears, it must return with more sublime image; and if it sleeps, it must dream of a better awakening, for it is ever greater upon its rebirth.

Had I filled myself with all that you know, what room should I have for all that you do not know?

How noble is the sad heart who would sing a joyous song with joyous hearts.

I love you, my brother, whoever you are – whether you worship in your church, kneel in your temple, or pray in your mosque. You and I are all children of one faith, for the divers paths of religion are fingers of the loving hand of one Supreme Being, a hand extended to all, offering completeness of spirit to all, eager to receive all.

If you can see only what light reveals and hear only
what sound announces,
Then in truth you do not see nor do you hear.

Inspiration will always sing; inspiration will never explain.

Many a doctrine is like a window pane. We see truth through it, but it divides us from truth.

Learning is the only wealth tyrants cannot despoil. Only death can dim the lamp of knowledge that is within you. The true wealth of a nation lies not in its gold or silver but in its learning, wisdom, and in the uprightness of its sons.

Remember, one just man causes the Devil greater affliction than a million blind believers.

Spiritual awakening is the most essential thing in man's life, and it is the sole purpose of being. Is not civilisation, in all its tragic forms, a supreme motive for spiritual awakening? Then how can we deny existing matter, while its very existence is unwavering proof of its conformability into the intended fitness? The present civilisation may possess a vanishing purpose, but the eternal law has offered to that purpose a ladder whose steps can lead to a free substance.

The heart's affections are divided like the branches of the cedar tree; if the tree loses one strong branch, it will suffer but it does not die. It will pour all its vitality into the next branch so that it will grow and fill the empty place.

The truly good is he who is one with those who are deemed bad.

They deem me mad because I will not sell my days for gold;
And I deem them mad because they think my days have a price.

We live only to discover beauty. All else is a form of waiting.

When you reach the end of what you should know, you will be at the beginning of what you should sense.

You cannot have youth and the knowledge of it at the same time;

For youth is too busy living to know, and knowledge is too busy seeking itself to live.

All things in this creation exist within you, and all things in you exist in creation; there is no border between you and the closest things, and there is no distance between you and the farthest things, and all things, from the lowest to the loftiest, from the smallest to the greatest, are within you as equal things. In one atom are found all the elements of the earth; in one motion of the mind are found the motions of all the laws of existence; in one drop of water are found the secrets of all the endless oceans; in one aspect of you are found all the aspects of existence.

Between the frown of the tiger and the smile of the wolf the flock is perished; the ruler claims himself as king of the law, and the priest as the representative of God, and between these two, the bodies are destroyed and the souls wither into nothing.

Every seed is a longing.

How often have I attributed to myself crimes I have never committed, so that the other person may feel comfortable in my presence.

I once heard a learned man say, "Every evil has its remedy, except folly. To reprimand an obstinate fool or to preach to a dolt is like writing upon the water."

If you do not understand your friend under all conditions you will never understand him.

Is there a greater fault than being conscious of the other person's faults?

Learning nourishes the seed but it gives you no seed of its own.

Money is like love; it kills slowly and painfully the one who withholds it, and it enlivens the other who turns it upon his fellow men.

Only great sorrow or great joy can reveal your truth. If you would be revealed you must either dance naked in the sun, or carry your cross.

Remembrance is a form of meeting.

Strange that we all defend our wrongs with more
vigour than we do our rights.

The life that the rich man spends in heaping up gold is in truth like the life of the worms in the grave. It is a sign of fear.

The people of the city feign great
Wisdom and knowledge, but their
Fancy remains false forever, for
They are but experts of imitation.

They say to me, "Should you know yourself you would know all men."

And I say, "Only when I seek all men shall I know myself."

We often borrow from our to-morrows to pay our debts to our yesterdays.

An eternal hunger for love and beauty is my desire;
I know now that those who possess bounty alone are
naught but miserable, but to my spirit the sighs of
lovers are more soothing than music of the lyre.

Between the spiritual world and the world of substance there is a path upon which we walk in a swoon of slumber. It reaches us and we are unaware of its strength, and when we return to ourselves we find that we are carrying with our real hands the seeds to be planted carefully in the good earth of our daily lives, bringing forth good deeds and words of beauty. Were it not for that path between our lives and the departed lives, no prophet or poet or learned man would have appeared among the people.

Every thought I have imprisoned in expression I must free by my deeds.

How stupid is he who would patch the hatred in his eyes with the smile of his lips.

He who endeavours to cleave the body from the spirit, or the spirit from the body, is directing his heart away from truth. The flower and its fragrance are one, and the blind who deny the colour and the image of the flower, believing that it possesses only a fragrance vibrating the ether, are like those with pinched nostrils who believe that flowers are naught but pictures and colours, possessing no fragrance.